White Animals

by Teddy Borth

ABDO
ANIMAL COLORS
Kids

abdopublishing.com

Published by Abdo Kids, a division of ABDO, PO Box 398166, Minneapolis, Minnesota 55439.

Copyright © 2015 by Abdo Consulting Group, Inc. International copyrights reserved in all countries. No part of this book may be reproduced in any form without written permission from the publisher.

Printed in the United States of America, North Mankato, Minnesota.

102014

012015

Photo Credits: iStock, Seapics.com, Shutterstock

Production Contributors: Teddy Borth, Jennie Forsberg, Grace Hansen

Design Contributors: Laura Rask, Dorothy Toth

Library of Congress Control Number: 2014943704

Cataloging-in-Publication Data

Borth, Teddy.

 White animals / Teddy Borth.

   p. cm. -- (Animal colors)

ISBN 978-1-62970-698-6 (lib. bdg.)

Includes index.

1. Animals--Juvenile literature.   I. Title.

590--dc23

                    2014943704

Table of Contents

White

Color starts with white.
Inks and paints are added to
make other colors. Mixing a
color with white will lighten it.

Mixing Colors

● + ◯ = ●

● + ◯ = ●

● + ◯ = ●

● + ◯ = ●

Primary Colors

● Red
◯ Yellow
● Blue

Secondary Colors

● Orange
● Green
● Purple

5

White on Land

Polar bears have great noses.

They can smell a seal under

3 feet (1 m) of snow and

1 mile (1.6 km) away!

Arctic wolves have white fur. They live far north. They can live in -60°F (-51°C) cold.

9

Stoats turn white in winter.

The farther north they live

the more white they turn.

11

Silkie chickens are white and fluffy. Their feathers feel like silk. They cannot fly.

White in Air

Male snowy owls are mostly white. Females have more black markings.

15

Doves are known for their

beautiful white feathers.

They are signs of **peace**.

16

White in Water

Beluga whales are white.

This helps them hide in ice caps.

They hide from polar bears.

Betta fish are raised to be different colors. White is a popular color. Bettas are generally brown in nature.

More Facts

- Some animals can be born all white. They are known as **albino**. Albinos are very uncommon.

- Many white animals live where there is snow. This allows them to hide easily. Stoats live where there is no snow in the summer. They change from white to brown after winter. Now they can hide in the dirt!

- White is the color of light, cleanliness, and beginnings.

Glossary

albino – a person or animal without the ability for skin, feathers, or fur to show color. The person or animal will be all white.

peace – a time of no fighting.

primary color – a color that cannot be made by the mixing of other colors.

secondary color – a color resulting from mixing two primary colors.

23

Index

abdokids.com

Use this code to log on to abdokids.com and access crafts, games, videos, and more!

Abdo Kids Code:
AWK6986